THE UNVEILING

Trials, Tragedies and Transitions of a Child of God

Neisha A. Sibley

THE UNVEILING. Copyright © 2022. Neisha A. Sibley. All Rights Reserved.

Printed in the United States of America.

No portion of this book may be reproduced, stored in a retrieval system, or transmitted in any form or by any means, except for brief quotations in printed reviews, without the prior written permission of DayeLight Publishers or Neisha A. Sibley.

Published by

DAYELight
PUBLISHERS

ISBN: 978-1-958443-10-1 (paperback)

Dedication

I thank Christ Jesus our Lord, who has given me strength to do His work. He considered me trustworthy and appointed me to serve Him. (1 Timothy 1:12 - NLT).

I dedicate this book to young Christians, particularly teens, tertiary students, and young adults who may be going through a rough season and are wondering when it will be over; and those who are on the verge of giving up, thinking life cannot get any better, even though they are serving God faithfully.

This book is also for backsliders and those who are yet to find Christ, to encourage them that with the help of God, this journey of Christendom is doable despite being filled with trials, tragedies, and transitions.

Acknowledgments

This journey has certainly been a memorable one, and as such, I would like to say a hearty thank you to everyone who played a part.

First, I want to thank God for endowing me with such a task and for giving me the strength and resilience to pull through with writing this book.

Secondly, I want to thank Gizel Townsend, my friend and sister in Christ, who has been very instrumental throughout this journey.

I also want to thank my aunt, Cavaline Colquhoun, and my pastor, Reverend Dr. Ajilon Ferdinand, for their words of encouragement and support.

Last but not least, thank you, Crystal Daye and the DayeLight Publishing team, for helping to make my dream a reality.

Heaven bless you all.

Foreword

You are going to love this book—whether it is your first book purchase or the twentieth—because you can immediately connect with the author's experiences and apply the life-changing lessons in your walk with Jesus.

Many of us either learned what we know today from peoples' mistakes or our very own. Jesus said, "If any man should follow me, let him take up His cross." Firstly, there is an invitation to follow Jesus. Secondly, Jesus tells us there is a price to walk with Him. The price is carrying the cross. When you accepted the cross, you said yes to being different, you said yes to the wilderness, you said yes to rejection, you said yes to the process, and you said yes to waiting on God. This walk with Christ is not a walk in the park, it is not a one, two, three... It comes with trials, and tragedies that promise to lead to transitions.

In the Unveiling, Neisha intentionally uses her personal experiences and lessons learnt to give hope to those who feel alone, out of place or discouraged. In each chapter, Neisha shares deep and vulnerable

Foreword

content that you will connect with while having a sense of appreciation for your own journey.

As you read this book, you will realize that you can move beyond anything you have experienced and will experience in your life.

—Gizel C. Townsend

Table of Contents

Dedication iii
Acknowledgments v
Foreword vii
Introduction 11
Chapter One: The Call 13
    Lessons Learned 18
Chapter Two: Staggering at the Promise 21
    Prophecy Defying Reality 25
    Defying Realities 27
Chapter Three: Psychology, Eviction, and Depression 31
    Eviction and Depression 34
    Lessons Learned 38
Chapter Four: From Hustle to Entrepreneurship 39
    Lesson Learned 42
    With Purpose Comes Problems 43
    Entrepreneurship 45
Chapter Five: The Unforeseen Transition 49
    Lesson Learned 53
Chapter Six: Fired Up or Getting Fired? 57
    Lessons Learned 61
Chapter Seven: Manifestation Through Maximum Discomfort . 63
Additional Notes 69

References	71
About the Author	73

Introduction

"Sometimes your innate desire to chart your own path may result in innumerable mistakes. Nevertheless, you must chart on with the lesson you've learned from every single one." —Neisha A. Sibley

Growing up, I always wondered why I was so strong-willed. I would be the person to take another path even when the majority were going in the opposite direction. My colleagues used to laugh at me and say I was crazy because of my decisions to chart an unpredicted path, but I did not mind being different. I have been different all my life. As a result, I have had some really tough days of people misunderstanding me. I have been misjudged, mismanaged, and, like Joseph, I have been placed in prison-like situations for things I did not do. However, these experiences have contributed to the person I am today.

I have been a writer since I was a little girl; I think my mother could have predicted this venture. As a curious child, I remember reading books belonging to my older siblings, which overtime helped to

Introduction

develop my vocabulary and broaden my scope of knowledge. Writing was how I expressed myself; it was my outlet when no one seemed to understand me. However, throughout my life, I have seen where the Lord would have carefully compiled the chapters of this book which I have now written.

The Unveiling is a powerful book that consists of the many real-life, unfiltered experiences I have encountered. Notwithstanding, these experiences are associated with scriptures that tell a story of hope. Within this book, one can expect to see the mistakes we sometimes make as Christians and the correct approach that should be taken. In each chapter, The Unveiling unravels the continuous growth of the author and shows the importance of obedience to the manifestation of God's promises.

The Unveiling contains deep, vulnerable content that will connect readers to the power of their individual stories and how important it is for the journey they are currently on. This book ultimately epitomises Ecclesiastes 3:11, which in short says that the Lord makes everything beautiful in His time. I hope you will have a great read.

God bless you.

Chapter One
The Call

The Call

Unlike other Christians who would have been prophesied to at the altar, I was simply instructed in the form of a dream but confirmed years later. It was in November 2014, I went to bed that night and got the weirdest dream. In the dream the Lord spoke to me through the form of an authoritative figure; my former college lecturer.

It appeared as if I was in a classroom during an evening class. Everyone in the class looked like my schoolmates from high school. While sitting in the class, I could hear chatter all around me, but I was not talking because the lecturer had left the classroom to return. I did not know at what point she would return so I kept quiet. However, when the lecturer returned, a well-known classmate who was sitting directly behind me was still talking, so I turned around to hear what she was saying, and before I knew it, my lecturer called me out with a few others. I thought we were going to be punished.

When she had finished telling the other students what their sanctions were, I became nervous because I did not know what she was going to tell me to do. I wanted to explain to her that I was not talking but did not get the chance to do so. Suddenly I heard, "Neisha! I am sending you to Manchester to do

Chapter One

Ministry." I was startled. At that time I did not know what ministry meant. The dream ended with me walking to the bus stop across from the college campus to catch the next bus to go to Manchester.

As a nineteen-year-old, waking up from that dream was most confusing. I went to my grandfather and explained the dream to him and his response was, "Neisha, I know yuh going to preach in Jesus' name." I laughed because dada always had hopes of his children and grandchildren following in his footsteps. The following Sunday, I went to my pastor and explained the dream to her and she encouraged me to pray about it.

In my head I thought ministry only meant preaching, so the idea of ministry weighed heavily on me, and I was most resistant. Unknown to me was that ministry meant serving whether in music ministry, ministry in arts, evangelical ministry, or other ministries. As time progressed, I became involved in music ministry. I served in praise and worship ministry, and directed the children and youth choirs. I will admit that during this time I was not the best of singers. I struggled with pitch and staying on key but I was involved in the ministry and I loved what I did.

The Call

A few years later I moved to Kingston and while living there I started visiting the Papine New Testament Church of God. I would occasionally visit the Kintyre New Testament Church of God since it was closer to where I lived. One Sunday in December 2017, I was at the Kintyre church and went to the altar for prayer. While at the altar, Pastor Mario Samuels started prophesying as the Holy Spirit led him, and he mentioned that the Lord wanted me to sing and not hide my talent. I felt relieved in a sense because though I loved music, I was battling fear and self-confidence so I would only sing at home where no one could really hear me.

However, after this experience, I could remember just being proud of myself and the talent the Lord had given me, to the point where I would sing every day. I was happy to know that the Lord wanted me to sing.

Living in a small apartment room, sounds were easily transferable. I can remember one day while cleaning and singing, one of my neighbours knocked on my door just to ask if it was really me singing or if it was a recording. She was impressed with what she heard and that made me happy. I would now sing at work all the time and my co-workers would pull their chairs next to mine just to hear me sing. Singing

Chapter One

helped me overcome so many difficult seasons in my life and lifted my spirit on my worst days. Singing became my therapy; it also ushered me into the presence of God, so I could not take it lightly.

Returning to the Papine New Testament Church in early 2018, I was deeply moved by a sermon Pastor Michael Bradley had preached that morning regarding the need for labourers in the kingdom. I felt convicted by the word so after church I went to offer my service in the different ministries; I joined the choir and later, the praise team.

Joining the praise team was the beginning of an emotional and spiritual turmoil in my life. I struggled because, sad to say, I was a country-minded church girl who was fully entrenched in the country culture of praise and worship. However, as time progressed, I adapted to the changes and was soon a lay praise and worship leader. This did not come without its challenges. Coupled with the feelings of inadequacy was the struggle to meet the expectations of others. I got demotivated by the criticism of others and dreaded doing praise and worship. In addition, it got to a point where I grew overly uninterested in putting on a show on Sunday mornings because I felt like I was being a hypocrite by singing that Daniel God surely will deliver, yet going home to almost nothing to eat and could not find a monetary offering to put in the basket Sunday after Sunday.

My disinterest towards praise and worship was misunderstood by many who looked on, and though I could have verbalised what was going on to my ministry leaders, I felt at that time that my story of lack was becoming a broken record, so I kept it to myself.

Lessons Learned

I had to learn that the call comes with its challenges and most times these are tests of our faith, our love for God, and even our very motive. It showed me that the fact that I was willing to give up because of what others thought, meant that my faith was not really anchored in Christ, and my motive was centered around man's approval and acceptance rather than giving God glory.

My advice to those who have had or are currently having similar experiences is to do a faith check, a motive check, and a relationship check. Ask yourself, "Who is my faith centered on? What is my motive for serving or doing ministry? What determines my relationship with Christ? Do I have a close relationship with Him?"

Whether you serve as an usher, altar worker, teacher, or other leader, there will be moments when the discouragement from others may cause you to question the foundation of your faith. It is okay to do a spiritual assessment by asking those questions, rather than making an impulsive decision that satisfies your lack of faith.

On the other hand, if someone thinks you are not doing a good job, do not give up; the call was not given by man but by God. I later realised that one of the reasons I lacked confidence in my talent was because I was leaning on my own strength and ability rather than the God who enabled me. If the Lord has called you to a particular ministry, allow Him to equip you, and when He has equipped you, be confident in Him and not in yourself. The Lord can even use the criticism of others to help build and equip you for greater service.

Additionally, I learned that my refusal to serve while experiencing personal lack showed that I doubted God's ability to provide for me during that period. Do not let this be your narrative. I am in no way

The Call

saying that it is easy to trust God in these times, but a large part of the faith story is believing without seeing. I encourage you therefore to press on through lack and nothingness. God sees you; He knows what you are going through, and He has a perfect plan. How much do you trust Him to carry out His work even when you are hard-pressed on every side?

Be assured that the challenges you face are working together for your good (see Romans 8:28). Stay in the ministry; be true to your calling.

Chapter Two
Staggering at the Promise

Staggering at the Promise

Romans 4:20 says: "He staggered not at the promise of God through unbelief; but was strong in faith, giving glory to God." (KJV).

The above-mentioned verse refers to Abraham, who was strong in faith and believed that the promise God had given him was going to be fulfilled despite his frailties. Sad to say, unlike Abraham, I staggered a lot at the promises given through the Word of God. This was due to my lack of faith in God. I tried to affix God to my past experiences as a little girl who would get what she wanted whenever she asked her dad. Though I am not an only child, I am the last daughter for both parents. I resemble my dad a lot, and I believe that because of this, whenever I would ask him for something I could always count on him to provide it. In other words, I grew up being (a little bit) spoiled by my dad.

Though years would have changed this pattern of getting what I wanted when I wanted it, I still held God and others to this standard and would be disappointed each time my expectations were not met. A faulty way to think, isn't it? I thought that if someone made a promise, the fact that they made it known to the other person meant that the fulfillment of that promise was imminent. In other words, I

Chapter Two

thought that if God was not going to fulfill His promises in record time, then He should not have made it known to me in the first place.

Therefore, when the Lord would speak to me in my quiet time after prayer, or through scriptures, songs and even people, I would anticipate it with excitement and SPEED but little did I know that I was setting myself up for disappointment. This was a wrong way to perceive God. It took me over a decade to come to terms with the fact that God has a set time for fulfilling His promises.

Usually, after getting a revelation from a scripture, I would feel so empowered and joyful in my spirit, but those emotions would soon dissipate because of my ignorance towards God's appointed timing to fulfill His promises to me. This created a mental battle. I would feel guilty and attribute this guilt to my sins, which led to me fostering doubts and ultimately becoming angry with God.

I became angry after reading scriptures of God's promises that said:

1. "And the Lord will make you the head and not the tail..." (Deuteronomy 28:13 - NKJV), yet

I was a college dropout and was jobless for years
2. "...and by His stripes I am healed" (Isaiah 53:5), yet I was struggling with severe eczema all my life.
3. "...yet have I not seen the righteous forsaken, nor his seed begging bread" (Psalm 37:25), yet I was given notice by my landlord as I could not pay my rent.

None of these promises seemed to have materialised in my life at the moment. In addition, I began to reason with myself about some personal promises the Lord made to me and somewhat managed to talk myself out of believing that God was even speaking to me. I started to question myself, asking if it was really God speaking to me or if it was me trying to promise these things to myself. This process brought about a lot of confusion. I had now disqualified myself from being worthy to receive any promise from the Lord.

As a result of the unfulfilled promises, I became angry with God and no longer read the Bible or prayed as I should. I disbelieved anything someone would say when they said, "And the Lord said to tell

Chapter Two

you..." even when they were not speaking to me directly.

However, I grew to learn that:

1. I should not compare my earthly relationships to my relationship with God because He is sovereign and will do whatever He wants, whenever He wants to (see Psalm 135:6).
2. It is never what I can see; this journey of serving Christ is a faith-based journey as mentioned in Hebrews 11:6, which tells us that without faith it is impossible to please God.
3. Although God has given me a promise, it will not come to pass with me sitting down doing nothing. I need to pray over it and work towards it with belief and faith (see James 2:14-17).

Prophecy Defying Reality

As children of God, we often hear mighty men and women of God prophesying and encouraging others. If you are a recipient of prophetic utterances, you can agree that in the moment you feel happy and empowered that the Lord has spoken to you. These prophetic declarations may have confirmed or brought more clarity to something you sensed the Lord was saying to you, or they may just be new knowledge. Whether it is a confirmation or new knowledge, prophetic declarations have a way of exciting us on one hand but can be so powerful that it baffles us and begs to question the possibility of it coming to pass.

Unlike the conventional way of receiving prophecy, most of the mysteries revealed to me were through my own prayer. Before I would have received a word over my life concerning future events by ministers, I found that the more I sought the Lord through intentional fasting and prayer that He would speak to me concerning the things that He wanted me to do.

The year 2021 was the most baffling for me. I started off the year with fasting as I was hungrier for breakthroughs in my life than I was for New Year's Day food. I can recall the Lord telling me to embark on fasting for months ahead and instructing me on how to approach fasting. My ears were very attentive to hearing from God, and today I can say that my fasting was not in vain. In the moment, while the ground was breaking to give way, I could not physically see it, but it all made sense afterward.

Chapter Two

Defying Realities

Being raised in a Christian home, I would see family members who got saved later turn away from the faith. As a result, I took on the personal mandate to pray for my family and, after years of praying for salvation and restoration, the Lord spoke to me concerning them. Though in reality it does not seem as if anything is happening, I am confident that ground is breaking in the spiritual realm and soon they will turn to the Lord.

The prophecies that I would own businesses, direct choirs, release songs, write books, teach, coordinate, lead, among other things, in the initial moment, did not seem to align with my reality. But today I can see the Lord putting things in place, and I am encouraged. I can admit that I was one of those persons who would first examine my competence, social connections, and resources to determine whether the prophecy would come to pass. The truth is, if I had all those boxes ticked, I would not need the Lord or a prophetic word to begin with. Therefore, it takes faith and obedience, not competence, for the will of the Lord to manifest in our lives.

Staggering at the Promise

Though our varying realities may seem to oppose prophecy, let us not stagger at the promise, as it is the Lord who will take us through when we take that step of faith.

Chapter Two

What are the personal promises the Lord has made to you?

_____
_____
_____
_____
_____
_____
_____
_____
_____
_____

What steps have you taken to align yourself for the manifestation of them?

_____
_____
_____
_____
_____
_____
_____
_____
_____
_____
_____
_____

Chapter Three
Psychology, Eviction, and Depression

Psychology, Eviction, and Depression

Zeal, excitement, and joy are a few words I use to describe how I felt after matriculating at the University of the West Indies in September 2018. I felt a sense of pride and accomplishment as it took me almost five years to regain the courage to go back to school. I last stepped foot into an educational institution in 2013 while I was pursuing an associate degree in natural science but could not continue due to financial constraints. However, it was now 2018 and I was accepted in the faculty of social science to read for a bachelor's degree in Psychology at the UWI Mona campus.

I was living the prophetic word spoken over my life in 2017. God came through and I was happy. I felt unstoppable; I already had high pursuit in mind. Everything seemed well except for the fact that I had recently quit my job to focus on school and was not on student loan. While this was the beginning of a new academic chapter, it was also the beginning of a new level of suffering. I had an abundance of zeal but no money. What I call 'My Job Season' was fast approaching.

During this season, I remembered uttering words to God, words used in the book of Job when he was met with a series of devastation in his family. I could see

Chapter Four

the pattern of non-achievement in my family where none of my siblings managed to graduate college/university, though all of us attended a tertiary institution. Though my older siblings went all the way to their final year in college, they were unable to complete their degree for some reason or the other.

Being very conscious of this generational pattern, I knew that my academic pursuit would break generational curses in my family, but I had no idea it was going to be the fight of my life. This pattern of academic setback or non-achievement was a demonic one and had to be broken. Therefore, when the Lord revealed that I would go back to school, the enemy was mad. The devil knew I was going to destroy a pattern he created in my family so his plan was to take me out at all costs.

During this journey I experienced a series of 'lack' that I did not know could have existed. Academically, everything was great, but financially, I was literally living each day by faith. Where I resided at the time was walking distance from the university campus, so transportation was not a problem until I started having late evening and night classes in the summer. What took me through the thick darkness after a 9 pm class was a prayer and my two feet. It was later in my final year that I learned of the campus bus, which was not always reliable.

Eviction and Depression

The first room I rented when I started university was located on the ground floor of a two-story house on Gordon Town Road. The landlord was located upstairs which was central to the entrance and exit of the property. Therefore, as a tenant, it was impossible to enter or exit the property without him taking notice. Not having a sustainable income, I was now behind on my rent, and oh how embarrassed I felt each time I had to pass the gate to go to church or to school. One week turned into two weeks and two weeks into a month without being able to pay my rent. As time progressed, my church family pulled together to help me with a month's rent, but this could not become a habit as the church had needs too.

Though I understood what my financial status was, I was still reading and preparing for examinations. In other words, I tried to suppress my financial reality in order to stay focused on my studies. While studying, frequent emails from the university reminding me of my financial obligations only made things worse. By this time I ran out of excuses to give my landlord as to why the rent was not paid, and one

Chapter Four

Sunday night after church I was given notice by my landlord to leave. I tried to stay positive, but my reality caved me in, and I found myself in a dark place.

As the exam season approached, I realised I was feeling ill. I did not understand what was happening. I started feeling a tightness in my chest; I could hardly breathe. I had to open my mouth to get oxygen. It felt like someone was suffocating me. Though I had a history of asthma, I knew this was not asthma. One evening after school I could remember just running out of my room to the grill to get some fresh air because I was literally suffocating. I later found out I was having a panic attack.

Depression was imminent. Following this event was a period of endless crying at nights, asking the Lord to take my life because I did not have the courage to take it myself. I would get upset when I woke up in the morning and realized I was still alive, and God did not grant my wish. I remember one day I was walking to Papine square, and my mind was telling me to walk out into the road. I felt that would have made the process a bit easier, but I lacked the courage to hurt myself. I sometimes refused to eat as a way to punish myself for what I was going through.

Psychology, Eviction, and Depression

I was sad, hurt, and angry. In my head, I thought dying was the only way out of the physical and emotional pain I was feeling. As a Psychology student, I never thought I would be one to suffer from depression, anxiety, suicidal ideation, and a panic attack.

I felt that all God did was to promise, promise, promise, but nothing really materialized. I hardly prayed because I honestly did not want to hear anything God had to say, but He was very present in my situation. Knowing that pain precedes purpose, the pain felt unending. Where was purpose? I felt like I was in a dark tunnel that had no end. Nothing made my situation better. I did not want anyone to pray for me; I stopped believing every word the Lord said about me to the point where I rejected the promises. I soon rescinded my statements after being convicted about it.

What I call an immediate transformation of mind happened one night while I was sitting on my bed. I could clearly hear the Lord instructing me to read Isaiah 49, so I did, and when I was at verse 15, something powerful happened. I heard the Lord explaining verses 15 and 16 to me in the way a visible

Chapter Four

person would. It was the most mind-blowing experience I have ever had.

One of the things the Lord said was, "Though it is possible for family to forget you, I cannot forget you. You are the work of my hands. I have written your name in the palm of My hand. It is imprinted on Me; therefore, it is impossible for Me to forget you." After that encounter, I jumped off the bed and started praying. I rejoiced that night as if I had received a million dollars. Though my situation had not yet changed, my mind was, and I felt free.

The Lord continued using the same scripture to reassure me throughout my journey at university. My reality looked the same, but my mindset was different and that caused me to feel more hopeful. I was able to sit my exams by the help of God and those He used to help me.

As I got closer to completing my studies, the spiritual warfare against my finances got worse. However, the Lord always came through for me. Sometimes it was literally hours before an exam that I would be running to the bursary to pay my tuition and then running back to get into the exam. As time progressed, members of my family assisted, and I received awards for book grants which went directly towards my tuition. I was also one of the scholarship recipients at my church. Also, a few confidants gave sacrificially to my tuition, plus I could always count on the constant help from PATH (Programme of Advancement Through Health and Education) which made a tremendous difference in the pursuit of my education.

Lessons Learned

Whatever the Lord says will come to pass no matter how long it takes. Isaiah 55:10-11 says: "As the rain and snow come down from heaven , and do not return to it without watering the earth and making it bud and flourish, so is my word that goes out from my mouth: It will not return empty, but will accomplish what I desire and achieve the purpose for which I sent it." (Isaiah 55:10-11 - NIV).

Chapter Four
From Hustle to Entrepreneurship

From Hustle to Entrepreneurship

On campus, graduation and orientation were events that students would capitalize on. As soon as I learned this, I did the same. Having no source of income, I had to find a part-time job, something that could accommodate my classes. I remember working multiple jobs in my first year of university. Since my classes were mostly in the evening, I had the mornings free to do a job or two. I started working with the University Alumni Association during graduation. This job was a temporary one and became non-existent as soon as graduation was over. Thankfully, I got a job shortly after through placement and career services to work for a Jamaican tour guide company, and if we know anything about the job of a tour guide, it takes a lot of traveling.

I can remember doing a tour in Ocho Rios one afternoon with the hope of returning to Kingston for my classes. Though I was excited about the tour, I was worried that I would not be back in time for class. After the tour, we took the highway back to Kingston but by the time I was on campus, my class had already ended. I was disappointed. I wanted to quit the job but did not know how I would be able to provide for myself if I did. I can even remember juggling a job as a babysitter some days. While the

Chapter Four

child was sleeping, I would be doing my assignments and/or studying. It took a lot out of me, but it helped to pay the bills.

In the summer of 2020, I decided to take summer classes. When I started these classes, I was unemployed and had just returned home to the country after the breakout of the coronavirus. However, not long after returning to the country, a family member and I had an altercation that resulted in violent threats directed at me, so I had to leave.

I can remember that Sunday afternoon just packing my bag and not knowing where I would go. I knew I could not return to my accommodation in Kingston because it was only available during school sessions. I remember just praying and saying "God, if it's even under a tree, I'd rather sleep there than stay in this environment." So after reaching out to a friend of mine, she welcomed me with open arms. Little did I know that the Lord had divinely ordained for me to be at this particular location at this set time. The favour that followed was unbelievable.

One night, after attending a tertiary student prayer meeting online, prayers were offered up for me to get a job. After the session ended, the Lord spoke to me and instructed me to write the lecture notes I had outstanding because in the coming weeks I would be busy and would not be able to write them again. The following week, I got a call from a friend regarding an online job. It was an administrative assistant role for a small company in the United Kingdom. I was so elated; I quickly connected with the manager, and the rest was history. Through this job, I was able to pay for my summer courses and save enough to rent a small room for myself.

Lesson Learned

Sometimes the Lord has to reposition us to bless us. In Genesis 22:9-14, Abraham took what he had to go where the Lord sent him. Holding on to hope, he was obedient to follow God's direction even if it meant losing his son. Did Abraham see another way out? I do not think so, but he got up and made the first step. It was then that the angel of the Lord showed up and provided the intended sacrifice. In addition, Isaiah 43:15-16 shows the Lord introducing Himself as the Creator of the universe; the One who specializes in impossibilities. It says: "I am the Lord, your Holy One, the creator of Israel, your King. Thus, saith the Lord, which maketh a way in the sea, and a path in the mighty waters." (KJV). The chapter continued with outlining the many wonders of God. God does

Chapter Four

not need to see a way in order to make a way. He is the way. I say this to say, DO NOT BE discouraged; your impossible situation is the perfect avenue for God to show up and prove possible. Take heart; you serve a way-maker.

With Purpose Comes Problems

Since I now had a stable job, I was not worried about the possibility of eviction. I was now living in the community of Tavern, literally five minutes from the university campus by vehicle. This room was attached to the landlord's house where he lived with his twenty-five-year-old son. Having lived there for a few months, I realised his son had frequent changes in his mood so I cautioned myself in my interactions with him.

Months went by before the landlord left to go overseas. I can remember completing my assignments one Sunday evening when a sudden power outage occurred in the community. This made the surroundings very quiet and dark. At that time, I had about 3% battery charge on my phone and no candle. Sitting on my bed, I waited patiently for the electricity to return. Suddenly, I heard a knock on the door. The fact that I did not hear any footsteps prior to the knocking, to me, was petrifying. I waited until the third knock and then asked who it was. To my surprise it was the landlord's son asking me to let him in so he could use my bathroom. After saying 'No!' his response was, "Why are you talking so loudly?" He knew the neighbours next door would know what he was up to if I spoke loudly, so he did not want me to speak. He already made his plan, so the electricity outage was the perfect time for him to launch his attack. That night I could hear the enemy clearly saying, "You are going to die tonight." A cloud of fear overshadowed me; my heart started racing, and I was confused.

My battery was dying, so I could not call anyone; the only thing I could do was to notify my church WhatsApp group so someone nearby could reach out. I was later assisted by some church members who had electricity in their neighbourhood. Having been rescued by my church family, I was able to complete the assignment I was working on so that it could be submitted. Looking back, I can see how the enemy tried in every way to destroy my life. He was bent on taking me out in whatever way he could, but I thank God none of his plans worked (see Isaiah 54:17).

Chapter Four

Entrepreneurship

I had now moved on from my previous online job and needed additional funds to sustain myself, so I started to sell jewelry (leather armbands) at my church. My mother had items that she would sell in the country from time to time, so when I reached out to her about my financial situation, she suggested that I sell them so I could help myself. Having never charted a path such as this, I was somewhat timid. Not knowing if anyone would purchase these items, I stepped out on faith anyway. After church, I would walk to Papine to sell to different vendors. During the week, in between classes, I would run to Papine to sell my armbands to taxi drivers. I would also go to business places such as pharmacies, supermarkets, and so on. At first, I was scared, but after receiving my first sale, it motivated me to continue. My church family would support me a lot; as a result, I started selling chocolate balls too.

Selling chocolate balls was a venture I ran with without second guessing. What motivated this venture was the vision I received. I envisioned myself designing labels for packaging, so I created the labels on my laptop and printed them. I bought staplers, paper bags, and other materials, and got started on selling my "Good ole Jamaican Chocolate

Balls." Though I did not make a lot of profit since I was almost paying the same price for them, I was however impressed at the finished work. My chocolate balls were always in demand as they brought back the good old days of making chocolate tea. When I looked at my chocolate balls, they were properly labeled, packaged and ready to go. I enjoyed every bit of this business venture. Today I can clearly see how the Lord had used that experience to prepare me for the businesses that He would instruct me to start.

Chapter Four

When was the last time you stepped out on faith to start something that has been laid on your heart? It could be a business idea, write a book, a blog, start a course etc.?

_____
_____
_____
_____
_____
_____
_____
_____

What was your experience like? If you have not yet started, when do you plan to start?

_____
_____
_____
_____
_____
_____
_____
_____
_____
_____
_____
_____

Chapter Five
The Unforeseen Transition

The Unforeseen Transition

As mentioned in chapter three, the year 2021 started out as a year that baffled me. One of the things I learned was that when we fast and pray, we call heaven's attention to our situations, and there is absolutely nothing God will not do for us once it aligns with His will. In January 2021, while in youth fellowship, we were given the task of creating vision boards. I remember just writing some things that I knew would take a lot of work to accomplish, but I was willing to see them happen, so I wrote them down anyway.

The first vision I wrote was to have a closer relationship with the Lord. I also wrote that I wanted to grow and develop in my music ministry, take driving lessons, successfully graduate from university, become financially stable, start my business, and travel. Interestingly, travel was the last thing added to my vision board. Though travel was the last vision on my vision board, it played a huge role in my transition.

I always wanted to travel outside my country, but the reality of it would scare me all the time. I was most hesitant because I had the idea that I would not have access to Jamaican food. Funny, isn't it? There is nothing like good Jamaican food. However, the Lord

Chapter Five

granted me an opportunity to travel. This was the genesis of my transition. I was now in a different country, and I soon started adapting to a new culture. Prior to this, I had only traveled to different parishes in Jamaica, so this was a big transition for me. With the Lord's protection, my aim was to fulfill my purpose and to please the Lord in my endeavours. However, I must mention that as children of God we should always be on our guard because with every blessing comes testing, and if we are not careful, the devil will try to convince us that our very blessing is a curse.

Upon arriving in the United States and settling in, the enemy started sending all kinds of temptations my way. I was here on a mission, and my aim was to get that mission accomplished and be on my way home to Jamaica. Having been in my comfort zone for a long time, I sensed that I was in a season that called for me to put into practice those things I believed and held firmly to. Was I prepared for the losses? I am not sure I was, but I was prepared to hold as tightly on to God as I could. Coupled with other contributing factors, I remember having to leave my job and place of residence because I was not about to give in to sin for a moment and displease God. I had to follow the example of Joseph and run for the sake of preserving

The Unforeseen Transition

my moral values, character, and salvation. I am sure many did not understand my motives at the time, but I thank God He gave me the strength to obey Him.

One would have thought that by being obedient to God things would have gotten better, but instead, they got worse. I later relocated to a family member's residence who was initially happy to welcome me there, but two weeks later, I was cursed out and disgraced by my very own family member. This experience was very new for me as throughout my life I could not remember anyone ever speaking to me the way I was spoken to. I was shouted at, and the things that were said to me appeared to be things that happened from my childhood that were still held against me.

I remember sitting on the floor that night crying bitterly. I did not know what to do or where to go. I started blaming myself for what happened, but after retracing my steps and re-evaluating the scenario, I could not see what exactly elicited such an action. It was the enemy who was at work, but God was up to something. What I found interesting was the fact that I could feel a shifting of the season in the midst of all that was happening. That night before going to bed, the Lord instructed me to read Psalm 24. He

Chapter Five

reassured me that I should not worry about where I would go but should just take solace in the fact that the earth is His and everything in it. It was not long after that the Lord provided a place of residence and a better paying job. One of the things the Lord said to me during this time was "People you don't know will bless you, and it's not because of you but because I choose to." This resonated strongly with me when I saw how the Lord used people I did not know to come to my rescue. I did not lift a finger or pay a dollar to relocate; the Lord provided persons to offer their assistance.

Lesson Learned

Throughout life, we will have transitions. Some will come to test us, but in the end, it is for our benefit, such as strengthening our faith and personal relationship with the Lord. James 1:2-4 says: "Dear brothers and sisters, when troubles of any kind come your way, consider it an opportunity for great joy. For you know that when your faith is tested, your endurance has a chance to grow. So let it grow, for when your endurance is fully developed, you will be perfect and complete, needing nothing." (NLT).

My reminder to you, child of God, is to never underestimate the power of God to locate you in a

The Unforeseen Transition

difficult transition. Exert faith and keep your confidence in Him. Isaiah 43:2 says: "When thou passest through the waters, I will be with thee; and through the rivers, they shall not overflow thee: when thou walkest through the fire, thou shalt not be burned; neither shall the flame kindle upon thee." (KJV).

Chapter Five

Write down the times the Lord has located you in a difficult transition:

Chapter Six
Fired Up or Getting Fired?

Fired Up or Getting Fired?

To be fired up means to be on fire for God, to have fresh zeal and passion for the work of the Lord, to have spiritual excitement concerning the things of God, refusing to be bogged down despite challenges; always expanding exuberance toward the work of God.

Jeremiah 20:9 says: **"Then I said, I will not make mention of him, nor speak any more in his name. But his word was in mine heart as a burning fire shut up in my bones, and I was weary with forbearing, and I could not stay." (KJV).**

Jeremiah explained the hard work it took to be a mouthpiece for God. He mentioned that each time he opened his mouth to give a word, he was always met with criticisms and insults. However, what was more interesting was the statement that followed. Jeremiah admitted that even if he tried to keep silent, the word of God was like fire shut up in his bones. This description tells me that Jeremiah would have developed a lifestyle of exerting time and energy in the presence of the Lord. Being filled with God's word, it was impossible for Jeremiah to try and restrict the flow of God in his life. Jeremiah was on fire for God.

Chapter Six

Romans 1:16 says: **"For I am not ashamed of the gospel of Christ: for it is the power of God unto salvation to everyone that believeth; to the Jew first, and also to the Greek." (KJV).**

In Acts 9, we see the great transformation of Saul to Apostle Paul. Though Saul had great zeal for persecuting the church, after his transformation, the Lord channeled that same passion but in a different way. Paul was now zealous about preaching the Word of God. He was not afraid; he was not ashamed, and he sure was not keeping it a secret. Paul was fired up for the cause of Christ.

Esther 4:16 says: **"Go, gather together all the Jews that are present in Shushan, and fast ye for me, and neither eat nor drink three days, night or day: I also and my maidens will fast likewise; and so will I go in unto the king, which is not according to the law: and if I perish, I perish." (KJV).**

Trouble was imminent, but Esther remained steadfast in the Lord. She did not allow fear of the situation to allow her to lose her fire. Esther was not bogged down; she had been called to the kingdom for such a time; therefore, she could not ignore the needs of her people. Esther evoked the fire of God by exerting herself fully to fasting and prayer, and the rest was history.

Being a child of God did not exempt me from troubles as you can now conclude. It did not spare me from disappointments, trials, or persecution. Like Esther, I sought the face of the Lord through prayer and fasting, and the Lord responded in the most unconventional ways. I can remember getting fired from a job for no apparent reason. I was gossiped about by co-workers who had heard about the family dispute. I could not understand how a family issue could have implications on my job. I did not try to defend myself because the story was now twisted, and I was seen as the enemy. However, I was later hired as a professional in the educational field. In a few months I received commendation for my work ethic and was recognized by a parent who sent an email to the institution to make this known.

As time progressed, some of my co-workers became intimidated by my work ethic and started fabricating information about me. I can remember just shrinking at one point so they could change their misconception of me. That approach was wrong; I could not hide the fact that I was a passionate educator who loved to see things in order. The

Chapter Six

directors did not hide the fact that they despised me but, like Esther, I resorted to prayer and fasting. I was soon made aware of my termination. But as the lyrics of Rondell Positive's song states "I'm an overcomer, and I'm standing tall. I'm more than a conqueror even with my back against the wall."

Though I sought the Lord diligently, and though this was a job I loved, I was still fired. Unknown to me, I was becoming comfortable in an environment I was supposed to pass through. Being fired up for God requires alertness and readiness to move when He speaks. I questioned why He would grant me an opportunity and then take it away but rested in the fact that His ways are perfect.

Lessons Learned

There are so many lessons learned from this chapter in my life. Here are a few:

1. We should never become comfortable in an environment that we were meant to pass through.

2. Sometimes the Lord must shake the very foundation of our beliefs to realign our focus to His.

Fired Up or Getting Fired?

3. We should never shrink in order to cushion someone's insecurity.

With the third point in mind, I leave a very powerful poem with you.

"Our deepest fear is not that we are inadequate, our deepest fear is that we are powerful beyond measure. It is our light, not our darkness that most frightens us. We ask ourselves who am I to be brilliant, gorgeous, talented and fabulous. Actually, who are you not to be? You are a child of God. You playing small does not serve the world. There's nothing enlightened about shrinking so that other people won't feel insecure around you. We were born to make manifest the glory of God within us. It's not just in some of us, it's in everyone. And as we let our own light shine, we consciously give other people the permission to do the same. As we are liberated from our own fear, our presence automatically liberates us."

—1994 Inaugural Speech by Nelson Mandela

Chapter Seven
Manifestation Through Maximum Discomfort

Manifestation Through Maximum Discomfort

Behold, I have refined thee, but not with silver; I have chosen thee in the furnace of affliction. (Isaiah 48:10 - KJV).

Similar to the process of gold purification, where it is passed through a series of high temperatures to be refined, the Lord uses the furnace of affliction to refine us.

There are three important scientific information about gold that will help us understand the importance of the furnace of affliction:

1. To improve the quality of the gold, it is mandatory that it undergoes the process of refining (Gittins, 2017).

2. The process of refining gold includes recovering it from its impure form and converting it through maximum heat to remove impurities (Burns, 2017).

3. The value of gold is connected to how pure it is (Bank, 2017).

Understanding the value of our furnace of affliction will bring us clarity and appreciation for the process. It is in the power of the Lord to choose whatever

Chapter Seven

means He wants; in the end, He will get the praise. Though those means may seem extreme, it is the Lord who determines them.

Once we accept salvation, the life that we live is now for the sake of Christ. Galatians 2:20 tells us that it is no longer we who live but Christ who lives in us. Matthew 16:24 reminds us that if we choose to follow Christ, we first have to deny ourselves and then take up our cross. Everyone has a different cross to carry; therefore, it is necessary that we deny ourselves because without doing so we may end up denying the cross instead.

Let us be honest; we all love ourselves. Therefore, I do not believe it is the desire of any of us to deliberately cause ourselves hurt or pain. Rather, our natural response is to protect ourselves from impending danger. Even security guards, whose job requires that they protect the lives of others, have the natural inclination to first protect themselves. This shows us that the call to be a true child of God requires total dependence on God. Living for Christ does not only constitute trials and persecution; we must understand that the cross precedes the crown. In 2 Timothy 2:12, Paul, having understood the weight of the ministry that lies ahead of Timothy, encouraged him saying: **"If we suffer, we shall also reign with him: if we deny him, he also will deny us." (KJV).**

Ministry is easy when everyone is cooperating and unity is at its best, but when trials and persecution appear, it seems hard to carry out the work of the Lord. While Jesus was on earth, His ministry did not go untouched. People criticised and labeled Him and downplayed His sovereignty.

Therefore, manifestation cannot be achieved through comfort. In order to stretch us to the capacity He needs us, God has to sometimes make us uncomfortable through the furnace of affliction. We must be willing to abandon the very traditions that we have held on to for years.

Many of us desire so much more, but we are bound by the limitations of our minds which stem from culture and tradition. I would consider Jesus to be versatile. He never confined Himself to one way of doing anything. He performed miracles in different ways and healed the same sickness using various methods. Why then should we desire manifestation at our comfort level? There is so much more to you. God wants to pull us out of the ordinary, not only to

Chapter Seven

stretch us to our desired capacity but also for us to take the limits off Him.

Job, having lost everything in his life, endured his furnace of affliction in order to cultivate stronger faith and dependence on God.

But He knoweth the way that I take: when he hath tried me, I shall come forth as gold. (Job 23:10 - KJV).

In this verse it was clear that Job understood the mandate. He knew this process could only add more value to him and remove the presence of any impurities.

Ask yourself these questions: "Have I patiently endured my furnace of affliction? Did I withdraw in the process? Am I going through that process now? If so, what is my attitude towards the furnace of affliction? Have I allowed myself to be fully refined?"

Romans 8:19-23 says: **"For the earnest expectation of the creature waiteth for the manifestation of the sons of God. For the creature was made subject to vanity, not willingly, but by reason of**

him who hath subjected the same in hope. Because the creature itself also shall be delivered from the bondage of corruption into the glorious liberty of the children of God. For we know that the whole creation groaneth and travaileth in pain together until now. And not only they, but ourselves also, which have the firstfruits of the Spirit, even we ourselves groan within ourselves, waiting for the adoption, to wit, the redemption of our body." (KJV).

As creatures we earnestly wait to see the fulfillment of the promise. We walk around enduring the pain as pregnant mothers; we are undergoing spiritual contractions to deliver the gift and talents given to us. In our hearts of hearts, we know there is more, and we are determined to see it. As we undergo our final contractions associated with manifestation, let us be ready. The set time to manifest is now.

Additional Notes

References

Burns, T., Gittins, L., & Bank, E. (2019, March 2). *Refining systems used to make Gold Bars*. Sciencing. Retrieved November 28, 2021, from https://sciencing.com/refining-used-make-gold-bars-8085641.html.

The King James Bible, New Living Translation and New International Version

About the Author

Neisha A. Sibley was born in St. Mary, Jamaica, and has been a Christian for over ten years. She has served in various capacities at the Palmetto Grove New Testament Church of God in St. Mary, and later moved to Kingston where she became a member of the Papine New Testament Church of God. Neisha is a lover of music and finds her passion in writing and singing her own songs.

She is a recent graduate of the University of the West Indies where she pursued a Bachelor of Science Degree in Psychology and a minor in Management Studies. She is strongly motivated by a quote of her own that says, *"Sometimes our innate desire to chart our own path may result in innumerable mistakes. Nevertheless, we must chart on with the lessons we've learned from every single one."* In essence, Neisha believes in creating a path of her own, even if the entrance seems to be decked with countless obstacles.